GUARDING
SUPERMAX PRISONS

BY MADDIE SPALDING

Published by The Child's World®
1980 Lookout Drive • Mankato, MN 56003-1705
800-599-READ • www.childsworld.com

Acknowledgments
The Child's World®: Mary Swensen, Publishing Director
Red Line Editorial: Editorial direction and production
The Design Lab: Design

Design Element: Iaroslav Neliubov/Shutterstock Images
Photographs ©: Val Lawless/Shutterstock Images, cover, 1; Tony Dejak/
AP Images, 5; Elaine Thompson/AP Images, 6; Pascal Parrot/Sipa USA/
AP Images, 9; Eric Risberg/AP Images, 10; Jelson25 CC3.0, 13; Steve
Miller/AP Images, 15; Mark Reis/Colorado Springs Gazette/AP Images,
16, 19; Chris McLean/Pueblo Chieftain/AP Images, 17

ISBN 9781503808072
LCCN 2015958275

Printed in the United States of America
Mankato, MN
June, 2016
PA02302

ABOUT THE AUTHOR

Maddie Spalding is an enthusiastic writer
and reader. She lives in Minneapolis,
Minnesota. Her favorite part of writing
is learning about new and interesting
subjects.

TABLE OF CONTENTS

CHAPTER 1

No Escape

It was 1999. Bank robber Jack Powers was in an Atlanta prison. He had lived there for nine years. His friend had been killed by inmates in 1994. Other prisoners had threatened Powers.

The government had promised to reduce his 40-year sentence. But Powers had waited long enough. He took matters into his own hands.

Powers made a dummy that looked like him. He also made a hook. He slipped the dummy under his blanket. He slid through a prison grate. Powers used the hook to climb the side of the building. He jumped over a 16-foot (4.9 m) electric fence. Then he climbed a barbed-wire fence. He did this with cardboard taped to his body. It protected him from the barbed wire.

Powers escaped. But he was free for just two days. The police found him. They put him back in prison. In October 2001, Powers was moved.

The entrance to the Ohio State Penitentiary

His new home was the Administrative Maximum
Facility (ADX) in Florence, Colorado. There would be
no more escaping.

The ADX is the highest-security prison in the
United States. It is located at the foothills of the

Ted Kaczynski, one of the ADX's most well-known criminals, sent bombs in the mail that killed three and injured more than 20 others.

Rocky Mountains. But the more than 400 prisoners do not get to enjoy the scenery. Their **cell** windows are only 4 inches (10 cm) wide. Prisoners spend one hour a day in a small outdoor cage. The rest of their time is spent staring at gray concrete.

The ADX is a supermax security prison. "Supermax" is a shortened form of "supermaximum." Supermax prisons are more secure than all other prisons. Supermax prisons hold the most violent criminals.

The first supermax prison was finished in 1989. The U.S. Bureau of Prisons decided it needed a place for prisoners who were extra hard to control. Maximum-security prisons were not safe enough. So the idea for supermax prisons was born.

Prisoners have escaped from other types of prisons. But no prisoner has escaped from a supermax prison.

CHAPTER 2

The Birth of Supermax Prisons

In colonial America, people accused of crimes were held in jails before trial and punishment. Men and women shared cells. Jailers did not do much to protect prisoners. They had to pay for food, heat, and clothing.

A man named Benjamin Rush was upset with the jail system. He did not think prisoners were treated fairly. So he created the Philadelphia Society for Alleviating the Miseries of Public Prisons. This was the first group in the world dedicated to changing the prison system.

Rush met with society members in 1787. He shared his ideas for a better prison system. He thought prisons should give prisoners time to be alone. He did not think the system allowed that.

These days, Eastern State Penitentiary is a
U.S. National Historical Landmark open for tours.

Rush's ideas led to the creation of a new prison.
It was built in Philadelphia. It was called the Eastern
State **Penitentiary**. Eastern State opened in 1829.
It was a new kind of prison. It used a method called

Alcatraz Island is home to one of history's most famous supermax prisons.

solitary confinement. Prisoners were left alone for most of the day. The prison had 250 cells. The only book prisoners were allowed to read was the Bible. They were supposed to use their Bibles to pray and **repent**. Prison workers hoped prisoners would become nonviolent. But that did not happen. Many prisoners developed mental illness.

Eastern State closed
in 1971. Another
experimental prison
had opened in 1934
on Alcatraz Island in
San Francisco Bay.
This prison also used
solitary confinement.
But it was more extreme
than Eastern State.
The most dangerous
prisoners were kept
in D Block. D Block was a hallway filled with
solitary-confinement cells. Some did not have any
light. Others were soundproof.

Alcatraz closed in 1963. It cost the government too
much money to run. Alcatraz prisoners were moved
to other maximum-security prisons. One of those
was the U.S. Penitentiary (USP) Marion in Illinois.
The Federal Bureau of Prisons moved the nation's
worst criminals there in 1979. But USP Marion's

SPECIAL HOUSING UNITS

The U.S. Bureau of Prisons has different terms for "solitary confinement." They call cells where inmates are isolated "special housing units" or "SHU." SHU doors are solid metal. Each door has one nickel-sized hole. The SHU at Pelican Bay State in Crescent City, California, houses many different gang members. They have to stop all contact with their gang for six years to leave SHU. Guards monitor mail to make sure the rule is followed.

MURDER IN USP MARION

Tensions were high in USP Marion in 1983. Prisoners felt guards were mistreating them. Prisoner Thomas Silverstein was upset with guard Merle Clutts. Silverstein was guided from his cell on October 22 to take a shower. He was handcuffed. Another prisoner slipped him a makeshift handcuff key and a knife. Silverstein freed himself and killed Clutts. This event led to greater security at USP Marion.

security was not strong enough. Violence broke out. It was the worst in 1983. One prisoner and two prison officers were killed in the same week.

The Bureau of Prisons realized that security needed to be stronger. Maximum security was not enough. The bureau came up with an idea for supermax prisons.

The first supermax prison was Special Management Unit I in Florence, Arizona. It opened in 1987. Other states followed. Many supermax prisons were built in the 1990s. Some states added supermax units to existing lower-security prisons. By 2000, 36 states had built supermax prisons or added supermax units.

An aerial view of the Pelican Bay State Prison complex in California.

CHAPTER 3

High-Tech Security

Supermax prisons hold highly dangerous criminals. Some, such as Ted Kaczynski, are sentenced to them immediately. Others have escaped from lower-security prisons. Some attacked other inmates or prison guards. Supermax prisons need high security. Advanced technology is part of this security.

The ADX has the best security of any supermax prison in the United States. The building has 1,400 steel doors. Guards in control rooms open doors and gates remotely.

These guards also control other parts of the prison. They control how long inmates shower. They can control the amount of light in a cell. The controls do not allow two doors within a **pod** to be open at the same time. This keeps prisoners from interacting with each other. Video cameras are

A guard stands watch at the Northern Correctional
Institution in Somers, Connecticut.

also controlled remotely. The ADX has 168 video
cameras. Prisoners are under constant watch.

There is even more high-tech security outside
prison walls. All supermax prisons have **perimeter**
fences. These keep prisoners from escaping and
control who enters and exits the building.

Supermax prison security is a mix of high-tech features and more traditional tools such as razor wire.

Two or more fences surround a supermax prison. The inside fence is usually an electric fence. Other fences are topped with razor wire. An 8,000-volt electric fence surrounds the ADX. This fence sends a shock when touched. The shock can kill a person who touches it a second time.

There are guard towers circling supermax prisons. The number of towers varies. Eleven guard towers surround Pelican Bay State Prison. There are six towers around the ADX. These towers allow guards to keep watch from all sides.

The ADX uses attack dogs to guard the outside of the prison. The prison also features lasers and pressure pads. Lasers scan the perimeter. Pressure pads are thin sheets. They trigger an alarm when stepped on. Motion detectors and cameras also watch the outside of the building.

Supermax prison security serves two purposes. It keeps prisoners from escaping. It also protects staff. Supermax prisons are the most secure in the world. This is largely due to advanced technology.

These guard towers are just one of the many security features at the ADX.

CHAPTER 4

Prisoner Restrictions

Technology is an important part of supermax security. But supermax prisons also use prisoner restrictions as a form of security. Supermax prisons are designed to isolate prisoners. This keeps them from hurting guards or other prisoners.

Walking into a supermax prison for the first time can be shocking. One ADX prisoner compared it to walking into a tomb. The ADX's concrete walls weigh 5,000 pounds (2,268 kg) per square inch. They are crisscrossed every 8 inches (20 cm) with steel bars.

Supermax prison cells are uncomfortable. This is especially true for ADX cells. Most of the furniture is made of concrete. This includes beds, desks, stools, and TV stands. A thin foam mattress sits on each concrete bed. Anything that could be made into a

A CELL IN THE ADX

locking cell door

toilet

concrete desk

concrete stool

concrete bed

thin mattress

weapon is removed. This includes toilet seats and toilet handles.

The supermax cell itself has a special design. It is built so prisoners cannot see other inmates. They also cannot see much of the outside world. Supermax cells are between 70 and 80 square feet (6.5 to 7.4 sq m). This is the size of an average bathroom.

Each ADX cell has one narrow window. This window is about 3 feet (0.9 m) high. It is only 4 inches (10 cm) wide. It allows prisoners to see the sky but nothing else.

ADX cells also have two doors. The outer door is solid. This keeps prisoners from seeing each other. The inner door is barred. It has a small slot. Prison staff slide food trays through this slot. Medical staff also provide medication through it.

The average prisoner spends 23 hours a day in his or her cell. Prisoners are usually allowed one hour of exercise a day. Outdoor exercise at the ADX happens in cages. These cages are slightly bigger than the prison cells. A guard puts leg irons, handcuffs, and belly chains on inmates when they are outside. The guard then leads the prisoners to the exercise cage. This is the only human contact supermax prisoners have on a daily basis. Limited family visits are allowed. But prisoners are separated from their family by thick glass.

Whether this treatment is fair or not is an ongoing debate. Some human rights groups argue it is unfair. They have filed **lawsuits** against the Bureau of Prisons. Others think isolation is needed for such dangerous prisoners.

The future of supermax prisons is unclear. But one thing is for sure. Supermax prisons have created a high standard of security. No other type of prison has been able to match it. When a prisoner enters a supermax prison, he or she knows there is no escape.

GLOSSARY

cell (sel) A cell is a small room in which prisoners live inside a prison. A supermax cell has concrete furniture that makes it uncomfortable for prisoners.

federal (FED-ur-uhl) Federal buildings are buildings relating to the national government. The Administrative Maximum Facility (ADX) prison is the only federal supermax prison in the United States.

infamous (IN-fuh-muhss) An infamous person is someone who has a bad reputation. The ADX prison has many infamous prisoners who committed horrible crimes.

lawsuits (LAW-soots) Lawsuits are legal actions brought against a person or a group in a court of law. Some human rights groups that believe prisoners are treated unfairly in supermax prisons have filed lawsuits against the Bureau of Prisons.

penitentiary (pen-uh-TEN-chur-ee) A penitentiary is a state or federal prison for people found guilty of serious crimes. Supermax prisons can also be called penitentiaries because they house dangerous criminals.

perimeter (puh-RIM-uh-tur) A perimeter is the outside edge of an area. Perimeter security at supermax prisons includes fences and guard towers.

pod (POD) A pod is a group of eight prison cells. Guards make sure only one door in a pod is open at a time so that two prisoners in a pod are not outside their cells at once.

repent (ri-PENT) To repent is to feel sorry for your actions or behavior. Prisoners at the Eastern State Penitentiary were left alone for long hours in their cells with only a Bible in the hopes they would repent their crimes.

TO LEARN MORE

IN THE LIBRARY

Berne, Emma Carlson. *World's Scariest Prisons*.
New York City: Scholastic, 2014.

Gordon, Nick. *Eastern State Penitentiary*.
Minneapolis, MN: Bellwether Media, 2013.

Hyde, Natalie. *Alcatraz*. New York City:
Crabtree Publishing Company, 2013.

ON THE WEB

Visit our Web site for links about guarding
supermax prisons: **childsworld.com/links**

*Note to Parents, Teachers, and Librarians: We routinely verify
our Web links to make sure they are safe and active sites.
So encourage your readers to check them out!*

INDEX